Children Learn the Bible, Prayers and Other Readings

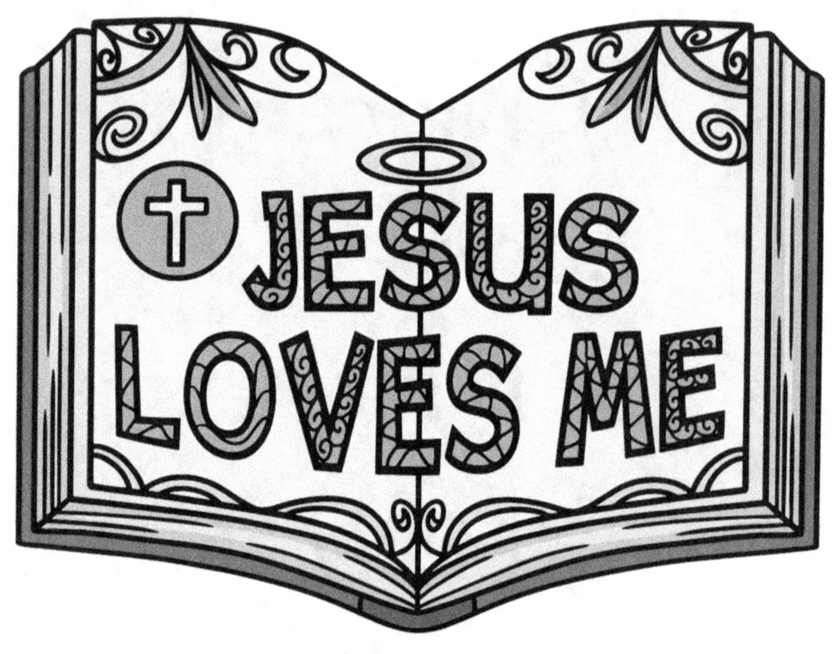

www.inspirepublishingco.com

Introduction

This book is an excellent choice for young readers who are beginning to explore the Bible. It provides an introduction to the Bible through verses in the bible that mention animals, teaching children about God's love, different prayers, and various aspects of faith. The book is filled with colorful illustrations, and it also includes easy-to-recite prayers and other engaging readings. It offers an immersive and entertaining learning experience for young readers, allowing them to deepen their understanding of the Bible in a fun and accessible way.

Table of Contents

Prayer is a Gift of God

PRAYER IS EFFECTIVE

Prayer is the ultimate solution for any situation in life

Thank you,
God, for today.
Please Bless all
my family and
friends today,
in Jesus's name.
Amen

GOD HEAR MY PRAYER

God in heaven hear my prayer, keep me in thy loving care. Be my guide in all I do, Bless all those who love me too. Amen.

- Traditional

SNAKES

Genesis 3:1-5

Now the **SNAKE** was more cunning than any beast of the field which the LORD God had made. And he said to the woman, "Has God indeed said, 'You shall not eat of every tree of the garden'?"

Don't worry about anything, but in all your prayers ask God for what you need, always asking him with a thankful heart.

Philippians 4:6

GOD HAS THE WHOLE WORLD IN HIS HANDS

HE HAS THE LITTLE BITTY BABY IN HIS HANDS

HE HAS YOU AND ME BROTHER IN HIS HANDS

HE HAS YOU AND ME SISTER IN HIS HANDS

PRAY
ALWAYS
NEVER
STOP

GOATS

Genesis 27:9

Go now to the flock and bring me two choice young GOATS from there, that I may prepare them as a savory dish for your father, such as he loves.

Trust in the Lord with all your heart; do not depend on your own understanding. Seek his will in all you do, and he will show you which path to take.
Proverbs 3:5-6

PIGS

Now there was a large herd of **PIGS** feeding nearby on the mountain.

Now, before I run to play, Let me not forget to pray to God who kept me through the night and waked me with the morning light. Help me, Lord, to love thee more than I ever loved before, in my work and in my play be thou with me through the day. Amen.

HORSES

Genesis 47:17

So they brought their livestock to Joseph, and Joseph gave them food in exchange for the HORSES and the flocks and the herds and the donkeys; and he fed them with food in exchange for all their livestock that year.

This little light of mine,

I'm gonna let it shine.

Ev'rywhere I go,

I'm gonna let it shine.

Jesus gave it to me,

I'm gonna let it shine,

let it shine, let it shine,

oh let it shine.

Dear God most high,

hear and bless Thy

beasts and singing birds:

And guard with

tenderness small things

that have

no words.

- Traditional

For I know the plans that I have for you,' says the LORD, 'plans for your welfare, and not for calamity, to give you hope and a future.

Jeremiah 29:11

DONKEYS

Zechariah 9:9

Rejoice greatly, O daughter of Zion! Shout in triumph, O daughter of Jerusalem! Behold, your king is coming to you;He is just and endowed with salvation,Humble, and mounted on a **DONKEY** .

Yes, Jesus loves me. The Bible tells me so.

An 8 second prayer!

"Lord, I love you and I need you, come into my heart, and bless me,

my family, my home, my finances, and all of my friends,

in Jesus' name. Amen."

REPTILES

James 3:7

All kinds of animals, birds, REPTILES and sea creatures are being tamed and have been tamed by mankind.

Prayer is sharing your thoughts, seeking God's guidance and expecting God's intervention.

LOVE
GOD

LOVE
PEOPLE

DOVES

John 1:32

John testified, saying, "I have seen the Spirit descending like a **DOVE** out of heaven, and it remained on Jesus."

"Evening, and
morning, and at
noon, will I pray,
and cry aloud, and
He shall hear me."

Psalm 55:17

PRAY FOR
EACH
OTHER
Amen to that!

Morning Prayer

Teach me now my
heart to raise
In a morning hymn
of praise;
And for Jesus' sake
I pray, Bless and
keep me through
the day.

- Robert Brett

God in heaven hear my prayer,
Keep me in thy loving care.
Be my guide in all I do,
Bless all those who love me too. Amen.

WHALES

Matthew 12:40

For as Jonah was three days and three nights in the belly of the **WHALE** , so will the Son of Man be three days and three nights in the heart of the earth.

Everything we do, the play, the work and fun You see it all and love everyone! So we meet today in this Sunday School, To learn about Jesus, 'cos you are cool! We love the stories we hear about you, Help us to listen and try to do. Teach us to grow and learn and love, Today we celebrate our Heavenly Father above.

Heavenly Father,
hear our prayer,
Keep us in Thy loving
care, Guard us
through the live long
day, In our work and
in our play. Keep us
pure and sweet and
true, In everything
we say and do.

RAVENS

Luke 12:24

Consider the RAVENS :
They do not sow or reap,
they have no storeroom or
barn; yet God feeds them.
And how much more
valuable you are than birds!

Oh, the Lord's been good
to me. And so, I thank the
Lord, for giving me the
things I need. The sun
and the rain and the
apple seed. The Lord's
been good to me. Amen

"Thank you God for the world
so sweet, Thank you God for
the food we eat, Thank you,
God for the birds that sing,
Thank you, God, for
everything!"

Lord, please guide us today in your strength and love. Help us all to avoid temptation, to grow in your likeness, and to trust you through Jesus Christ in all things. Amen

WOLF / LEOPARD

Isaiah 11:6

The **WOLF** will live with the lamb, the **LEOPARD** will lie down with the goat, the calf and the lion and the yearling together; and a little child will lead them.

Heavenly Father,
hear our prayer, Keep us in
Thy loving care, Guard us
through the live long day,
In our work and in our play.
Keep us pure
and sweet and
true,
In everything
we say and do.
Amen.

I have decided to
follow Jesus;

He gives me hope for each
new day.
I'm going to follow Jesus.

He lights my path all along
the way.
I'm going to follow Jesus

I will go wherever He leads
I'm going to follow Jesus

No turning back

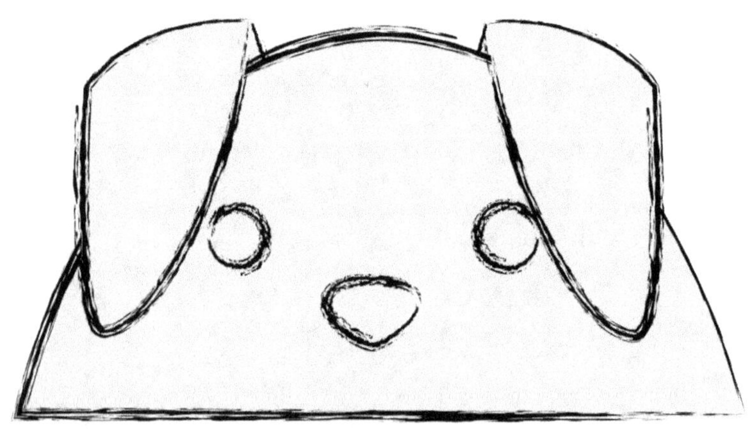

FISH

Matthew 13:47

"Once again, the kingdom of heaven is like a net that was let down into the lake and caught all kinds of FISH ."

When I see the moon
in the night sky,
I speak my evening
prayer;
Praise be to God,
For His kindness and
his goodness is
forever.

God is great and
God is good;
Let us thank him
for our food;
By His blessings,
we are fed,
Give us Lord, our daily
bread. Amen.

CALFS

Genesis 18:7

Abraham also ran to the herd, and took a tender and choice CALF and gave it to the servant, and he hurried to prepare it.

JESUS LOVES ME

THIS I KNOW

FOR THE BIBLE

TELLS ME SO

Prayer is like having a chat with God. It's a way for us to connect with someone who gets what we're going through and is there for us in our everyday life. It's a personal and close connection with our loving Heavenly Father.

LIONS

Revelation 5:5

One of the elders said to me, "Don't weep. Behold, the **LION** who is of the tribe of Judah, the Root of David, has overcome: he who opens the book and its seven seals."

THE GOLDEN RULE

To do to others as I would, that they should do to me, will make me gentle, kind, and good, as boys and girls ought to be.

GOD LOVES YOU, UNCONDITIONALLY! HE REALLY DOES!

Thank God we have Jesus and the Holy Spirit!

LOVE IS PATIENT

LOVE IS KIND

LOVE IS NOT JEALOUS

LOVE DOES NOT BRAG

LOVE IS NOT ARROGANT

SHEEP

Psalm 100:3

Know that the Lord he is God. It is he who has made us, and we are his. We are his people, and the SHEEP of his pasture.

God Made Every Day!

MONDAY

TUESDAY

WEDNESDAY

THURSDAY

FRIDAY

SATURDAY

SUNDAY

GOD IS LOVE!

Dear God,

Help us to focus on the greatest gift of all- Jesus. Thank you for sending your one and only Son, that we might be saved through Him. Amen.

RAMS

Genesis 22:13

Then Abraham raised his
eyes and looked, and
behold, behind him a RAM
caught in the thicket by his
horns

SMILE. JESUS LOVES YOU!

ELEPHANTS

Job 40:15

"Behold now, ELEPHANT, which I made as well as you; He eats grass like an ox.

i love Jesus

Today is a good day
TO COUNT OUR BLESSINGS

thank God we have Jesus and the Holy Spirit!

Jesus said: "I am the light of the world. Whoever follows me will never walk in darkness but will have the light of life."

John 8:12

DEER

Psalm 42:1

As the **DEER** pants for the water brooks, So my soul pants for You, O God.

We all have a friend in Jesus!

DRAW NEAR TO GOD

AND HE WILL DRAW

NEAR TO YOU!

-JAMES 4:8

Joy is putting Jesus and Others before Yourself!

J ESUS

O THERS

Y OURSELF

I Thank Thee, Lord

I thank Thee, Lord, for quiet rest, And for Thy care of me; O let me through this day be blest and kept from harm by Thee.

-Mary L. Duncan

ANTS

Proverbs 6:6-8

Go to the **ANT**, O sluggard, observe her ways and be wise, Which, having no chief, Officer, or ruler, prepares her food in the summer and gathers her provision in the harvest.

A thankful heart is a happy heart! Give thanks to the Lord, for he is good!

Psalm 118:29

Thanks to Jesus,

when God looks at me, he sees Jesus.

blessed. loved. saved.

THE LORD MADE TODAY, LET'S REJOICE AND BE GLAD IN IT!

Take your troubles to the Lord;

Cry out to Him and He will answer your prayers.

SCORPIONS

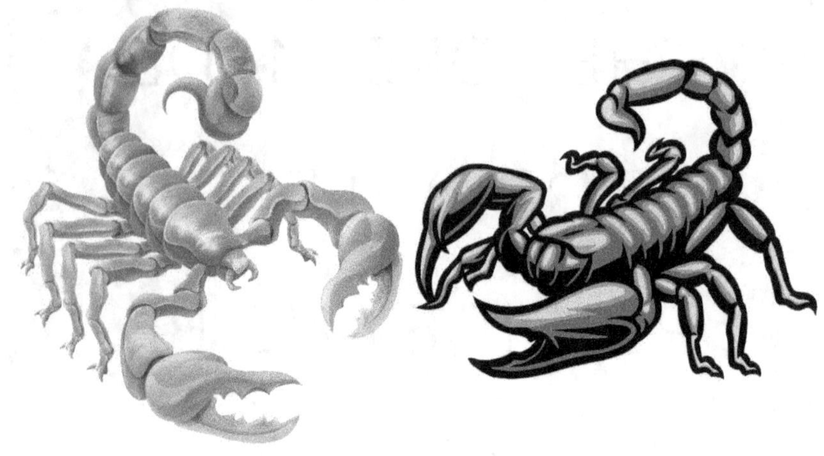

Luke 10:19

Verse Concepts

Behold, I have given you authority to tread on serpents and SCORPIONS , and over all the power of the enemy, and nothing will injure you.

JOY JOY JOY JOY JESUS JESUS
JOY JOY JOY JOY JESUS JESUS
JOY JOY JOY JOY JESUS JESUS
JOY JOY JOY JOY JESUS JESUS
JOY JOY JOY JOY JESUS JESUS
JOY JOY JOY JOY JESUS JESUS
HOPE HOPE HOPE JESUS JESUS
HOPE HOPE HOPE JESUS JESUS
HOPE HOPE HOPE JESUS JESUS
HOPE HOPE HOPE JESUS JESUS
HOPE HOPE HOPE JESUS JESUS
HOPE HOPE HOPE JESUS JESUS
HOPE HOPE HOPE JESUS JESUS
LOVE LOVE LOVE JESUS JESUS
LOVE LOVE LOVE JESUS JESUS
LOVE LOVE LOVE JESUS JESUS
LOVE LOVE LOVE JESUS JESUS
LOVE LOVE LOVE JESUS JESUS
LOVE LOVE LOVE JESUS JESUS
LOVE LOVE LOVE JESUS JESUS
LOVE LOVE LOVE JESUS JESUS
JESUS JESUS

God Loves You!

The Bible says, "God so loved the world that He gave His one and only Son, that whoever believes in Him shall not perish, but have eternal life"